To Forget Venice

PHOENIX POETS

PEG BOYERS

To Forget Venice

THE UNIVERSITY OF CHICAGO PRESS

Chicago & London

PEG BOYERS is executive editor of *Salmagundi*. She teaches poetry at Skidmore College and at the New York State Summer Writers Institute. Her previous books include *Hard Bread* and *Honey with Tobacco*, both published by the University of Chicago Press.

The University of Chicago Press, Chicago 60637
The University of Chicago Press, Ltd., London
© 2014 by The University of Chicago
All rights reserved. Published 2014.
Printed in the United States of America

23 22 21 20 19 18 17 16 15 14   1 2 3 4 5

ISBN-13: 978-0-226-18126-4 (paper)
ISBN-13: 978-0-226-18143-1 (e-book)
DOI: 10.7208/chicago/9780226181431.001.0001

Library of Congress Cataloging-in-Publication Data
Boyers, Peggy, 1952– author.
    To forget Venice / Peg Boyers.
        pages ; cm—(Phoenix Poets)
    Poems.
    Includes bibliographical references.
    ISBN 978-0-226-18126-4 (pbk. : alk. paper) —
ISBN 978-0-226-18143-1 (e-book)   1. Venice (Italy)—
Poetry. I. Title. II. Series: Phoenix poets.
    PS3602.O94T6 2014
    811'.54—dc23

                              2014002921

♾ This paper meets the requirements of ANSI/NISO Z39.48-1992 (Permanence of Paper).

To my sister Titi, who first gave me Venice,
and to my husband Robert and our children:
Gabe and Drew, Zack and Rachel, Lowell and Eileen

CONTENTS

ACKNOWLEDGMENTS

Poems in this book have previously appeared, some in different versions, in the following publications:

Harvard Review: "Mrs. Casanova"
H.O.W. Journal: "The Jewish Cemetery, Lido" and "Wall Moss"
Hudson Review: "Urn"
Inertia: "Lido"
Jai-Alai Magazine: "To Forget Venice"
New Republic: "Scirocco: *Otello* in Venice"
Notre Dame Review: "Ambition of Sand"
Paris Review: "At the Guggenheim Museum, Venice"
Poetry International: "Rooftop: Aerial View" and "Brodsky at San Michele"
Raritan: "Tadzio's Mother," "Titian's Magdalena Speaks from Lazzaretto Nuovo, 1576," and "Fondamente Nove"
Sewanee Review: "Crossing"
Southwest Review: "Callas in Venice"

I

SCIROCCO: *OTELLO* IN VENICE

Sandy heat of summer,
each putrid grain imbedded in sweat:

no breeze
in the courtyard of Palazzo Ducale

where mother's perfume almost obliterates
the Venetian stench. Powdered and scented, we

ready for the open-air opera, my mother and I, and Mario
poised between us

as winds and strings intimate
the coming storm

and stage lights crash over the grand marble staircase,
inaugurating the season of deceit.

In the dark Mario's expert fingers
forage in the folds of mother's skirt.

Cymbals and drums
confirm it all.

We follow the Moor who in his innocence
believes himself a cuckold but is not
while my absent father in his innocence
trusts and is betrayed.

I am evil
      because I am a man

sings Iago
that summer night in 1965,

the Istrian stone gleaming
pure under the stars.

      Dio crudel,
keep me silent—

to Iago's god I pray:
      Keep father safe in Sumatra

with no one to lead him
      to the Venetian light.

THE RUSKINS

I. JOHN RUSKIN CONFRONTS THE REAL FEMALE NUDE
(APRIL 10, 1847)

I pictured my virgin naked, *genuinely* naked,
baby smooth, Carrara white,

and hairless. Acceptable, I imagined, a patch
of delicate down here
and there, preferably blonde, nearly invisible.

And if on her body, sparse. And her hair,
the girlish blonde hair of which I'd dreamed,
would properly be confined to her cherub head.

But no! My bride was brunette!
To her credit, she was considerate of my preference and
chastely pulled the dark hair on her head into a matronly knot

at the nape, often concealing it all
with dainty lace.
But there was nothing to be done

about the pubis
sprawled on the bed, its lips gaping open
as if to mock me.

Hideous kinks of black wire coated
the so-called mons veneris—the mound I had pictured *nude*.
This—this vile hump—was *clothed*, draped

with a thick cape of black wooly hair, darker
still against the purity of our nuptial sheets.
Instead of the fine little-girl vellus,

a gentle slit opening to receive me,
bristles greeted my innocent member
and rendered me limp.

The portal to the womb was thus revealed:
a mass of oozing red folds, thatched over, wooded—
so like, yet unlike, a man's rank crotch!

Was there no virtue at all in it, you might ask?

Yes, one: when at last she stood up from her reclining pose,
hair covered the hateful vulva
like a merkin, veiled utterly the labial vestibule.

Looking higher up the trunk and away, for relief,
I found none. For under both arms hung
yet two more disgusting nappy beards!

And the stench of it all.
Apes, they say, attract
each other with such smells, but

nothing
could repel me more than her sewer
with its black grate of fetid tangles.

And, worst of all, the slimy stink pit bled!
What monster menstruates on its wedding night?
I ask you.

2. EFFIE GRAY RUSKIN WRITES TO HER MOTHER ON CHRISTMAS EVE, 1850

Dearest Mama: Eel! I am to eat eel.

At Casa Bembo, we shall celebrate
Christmas Eve at the very table where Lucrezia Borgia
often ate. The fare?
Risotto de la Visilia,

the principal ingredient of which is
—horrifying, but true
—eel.

All day the Romanists, who abstain
from meat on holidays, have been buying
up the eel at Rialto. From my window overlooking
the market I saw a perfect *lake* of blood spread

black across the stone ground
as aproned mongers lopped off
the heads of eel after eel, flinging

the wretched beasts, still
twitching, into the shopping bags
of eager, festive customers.
Our man, Carlo, claims the fattest, tastiest eels

are at least twenty-five years old, that they swim
to our rivers from the Sargasso Sea.
Across the Atlantic. Imagine.

Our very own Brenta appears to be one such *rio*
where Carlo hunts them for sport by night
with lantern light if the moon's illumination does not suffice.
Carlo explained, in rather too gruesome detail,

how he threads a wire hook through the eye
of a still-breathing carp. When the eel bite the bait
he swoops down with his net, scoops them up,

and tosses them into a bag, which he then drags
along boat-side in water to keep the
poor caught things alive and writhing—fresh
until the dinner hour.

To calm them, he reaches down
to pet the panicked devils
as they leap and thrash in protest.

He insisted I do so, too, promising
that they will not bite—though they have
the most fearsome jaws and teeth, two sets of them.
And what an agreeable sensation it was to stroke

so smooth and wet a creature! The slime
that covers their bodies of sheer muscle made
this all the *more* agreeable. Astonishing, no?

Will I, then, put
the meat
in my mouth
when the time comes? That

will be—as they say here—*il colmo*.
Like a bride on her wedding night
I await   the moment   with dread

and excitement.   Please God,
let the meat be sweet!
Legend has it that Doge Andrea Gritti died
of overeating grilled eel on Christmas Eve in 1538.

I am forewarned.

John says not to worry and both of us send you
our deepest love,
Effie

TADZIO'S MOTHER

Too young to be a widow,
too old for the beach.
Out of place as these upright
palms, propped in their terracotta
pots in the hotel lobby.
Everywhere my reflection framed
in gilded *ottocento* mirrors, dissected
in a thousand chandeliers.

Multiplied but alone.
Black veil of mourning, you
cover only my official grief.
No garb marks the passage from
fertile tree to desiccated stalk.
My sons will grow
and go
without ritual.

Last year the eldest
was by my side, still a boy.
Now he sulks on the promenade,
plotting his escape.
His furtive hand slips
inside his swim suit,
controllandolo,
like a passport.

He stalks the *spiaggia*,
half boy, half man,
perfect body glistening in the sun.
Eyes of passersby drink him in while
his siblings build castles by the *capanna*.
My Tadzio stands apart on the pier,
a handsome *kouros* set against the sea,
waiting for sport—or better.

His frail hand rises and waves
not to me, but to another guest
obscured by the terrace awning.
His lips part in a coy half-smile
revealing teeth thin like mine, jagged
and stained from years of indulgence, dark
against his pale, idle skin.

MRS. CASANOVA

She has no inner life.
Instead, she will have secrets.
And, like him, a mask to cover them.

definition of seduce [handwritten annotation]

This is the plan: under the mask she will dwell,
keeping what is on her mind
to herself.

In her transparent world secrets are hard to come by.
She will have to make do with mundane
matters of little consequence.

About the migraine she had last night,
for example, she will not speak.
Nor let on she is embarrassed

when exposed before their guests about
the several political issues she always gets wrong:
the intrigues at court, the betrayals, alliances.

intellectually slaughtering [handwritten annotation]

She is embarrassed to have been embarrassed
by something so trivial.
She will hide that too. Under the mask.

Nor will she admit that she was hurt
when mocked before their young friend about the songs
she likes, especially when sung by that new castrato in town.

humiliating [handwritten annotation]

masks often hide dislocation

She will refrain from showing how much she minds
being contradicted about stupid facts like the difference
between poplar and cedar, which hardly exist in Venice anyway.

Her pettiness shames her yet she feels deeply wronged.
That these tiny wrongs begin to add up
and weaken her is disturbing.

In her weakness she feels, and *is,* unattractive.
Looking into her husband's eyes
she is confirmed.

Under her mask she notes that yes, compared
to their lovely young friend, she really is a crone.
A stupid, unhappy crone disfigured by unhappiness.

No wonder her husband recoils from her in this state,
preferring the attentions
of their lovely young friend.

She too prefers their lovely young friend
to her pathetic unhappy self. Under her mask
she will hide her humiliations

and in that dark airless place let them fester
and grow and from that spreading rot
accumulate something like

an inner life, a place in which to dwell
alone, privately,
in her misery.

In her barren world this sad notion
of fashioning a secret place of her own passes for
a creative solution and, for now, consoles her.

But she is not yet adept at using the mask.
It will take practice and discipline
to achieve the necessary mastery.

When she looks in the mirror to give it a go
her Harlequin reflection greets her
with peals of laughter

undermining at once her determined sorrow.
Perhaps tomorrow she can get serious about her plan,
try on Pierrot or Colombina, the shrewd slave.

Today she is too easily amused—
a ridiculous failure even at despair.

Et phrastic

TITIAN'S MAGDALENA SPEAKS FROM
LAZZARETTO NUOVO, 1576

He painted me plump and frankly less than penitent.
Before contagion struck us both.
Before my milky flesh erupted in pustules.

When I bled from the mouth they banished
me to the island named for the saint
who rose from the dead.

I wasted away soon and with the other carriers made
a grave of the *barena* where limonium grows
heathery along the salt banks of the *ghebi*.

Now my famous hair, still abundant and red, lies
caked around what were my breasts.
My skin's dissolved into the marsh.

My bones arrange themselves in lime,
armature with no mass. It's what I expected.
Hawthorn and ash wind their roots around my neck,

but I don't mind: my breath's long gone.
The mouth that breathed now clenches
a brick stuffed between my teeth

to keep me from rising to prey on others, suck
their blood, spread my disease.
Oh to be a vampire busy at night with the work of living!

In my fever, I wanted *nothing*, nothing
but the *end*. Solitude, emptiness.
Un bel niente.

Instead, there is worry, guilt, regret—call it *something.*
Call it a soul.
Not to mention the others, the other souls, all rotting

in their own piss and shit, soiling their bloody shrouds.
Tell the living: here in the mass grave where they throw us
there is no oblivion, no relief.

No heaven. No hell.
Even the nihilist romance was a lie:
There is no nothing.

TO LENIN FROM VENICE

October, 1908

Darling Volodya

You've just left and already I am missing you
and your new Italian ways. We were both enjoying
them too much; better that you are gone.

I keep remembering how you held us all
that day on the Riva degli Schiavoni
(how you held *me*), still bitter about the *schiavi,*

the slaves who built it, then extolling their descendants:
the fishermen, boat builders, netmakers, canal dredgers
and stonemasons—all needing our help—

Orrrrrrrganizzare, you said, in your Slavic Italian.
Orrrrrrrganizzare.
Those fierce injunctions thrilling us all,

—those wet, northern r's!—so oddly aristocratic-sounding,
the inadvertently upper-class accent perfect
for these haut-bourgeois Venetians!

Only yesterday we played chess on our balcony.
I moved my queen's bishop across the diagonal
to threaten your remaining knight while below us

the garbage collectors crashed bottles and trash into their barge.
You castled and laughed your peasant laugh, rubbing
your cruel Socratic brow, pushing your fedora back

to cover the baldness, even in this heat. When I asked,
"And what of the hoteliers and waiters, shopkeepers, guides,
chefs, maids, glassworkers—what of the gondoliers?"

you answered, *Kill them. They belong to tourists!*
"And what of the university—the historians, philosophers—the brains
of the city, the nation?," I persisted, playing out our usual exchange,

and you, reliably on cue: *Kill them. They are not its brains but its shit.*
And "What then of me, Vladimir Illych?" I persisted, and you,
as always brutally charming: *Stay away from me or die.*

"But, my darling, I am your wife!" said I, still playing the game,
moving my queen to stare down your king.
You threw a pawn in its path, sweet devil, and began to sing

Fuck art, fuck tourists, fuck your insipid lament.
Kill them all, kill them all,
the whole putrid ferment!

At our stalemate, my dearest,
you pretended elation,
near-defeat as close as you could stand to losing.

But you were never good at pretense.
Nor am I *pretending*
to long for you, here in this suddenly dull city.

Today, in my listlessness, I wandered quite by accident
into Venice's library as I followed the arches around
the square to the side piazzetta and into the open doors of the Marciana.

The marble vestibule drew me in with its stark simplicity, but I confess
the ornate halls upstairs filled with gilded codices
and incunabula did not at all repel me.

Other rooms contained shelves and shelves of literature of every kind
which anyone in Venice—anyone!—can borrow. A miracle:
the people have free books! As soon they will in Russia

once we prevail. I am studying how it is done. Our people—
we shall teach them to read!—will soon read their Tolstoy
and their Chekhov and their Marx.

And they will read *You*, darling, *You*.
If you ask me today *What is to be done?*
here is my answer : send for me at once!

All my love,
Nadya

WALL MOSS

It's said I cure madness.
Brewed over fire, I hurry births.
Wanted or not.

I dwell in the interstices
where rock meets rock, decisively
in-between.

Light, food, open space—they are
not for me. What I need I take from dust, in the dark,
on the sly.

Do you hunger for solutions that do not exist?
Do your appetites exceed your means?

Come, find me
along Rio Marin by the Zattere or
beneath Ponte della Maddalena—

Come, pick my ovoid leaves,
grind them with a pestle,
make of me a physic.

Come! Eat me. Come!
Believe my flimflam:
Cure yourself with my self!

Grow resourceful.
Become like me completely Venetian:
   cling to debris, favor ruin.

II

CROSSING

for Mrs. Sullivan

Your death was for the best, they
all agreed,
for the best.

In the photograph my plump parents raise
a toast to the camera—china and crystal sparkling
with the sequins adorning my mother's bodice.

My first cruise: from Djakarta
to Venice: thirty days of cards,
shuffleboard, dips in the ship's pool.

We loved our purchased boredom.
Our cabin was a dollhouse:
tiny furniture crammed

in make-believe space
for tiny people
like you Sullivans next door—

your husband and Karen
compact, athletic;
you, sickly small, wasting

your way toward invisible.
Something ghastly in that emphatic smile
stretched to the max, about to snap.

25

At the on-deck service
I failed to cry for you, then
cried at my failure.

Dry-eyed Karen slipped me a toffee
to cover our giggles
through the perilous *Agnus Dei.*

For the best,
the others murmured,
for the best.

Afterwards, poor lamb,
you slid into the China Sea
without a splash—

five-two and eighty pounds,
aphasic, sad
little mother.

The white sheet that was your shroud
lingered on the surface, unfurling,
then surrendered.

ARRIVATA
April, 1965

Here the sea ends, she thought
as the luxury liner glided into the lagoon,
leaving the Adriatic in its wake, past faded palaces

rimming the canal, past the anomalous park
and sinking cake-like ducal palace, its filigree façade
shimmering behind rows of tethered gondolas bobbing

alongside tilted candy-striped poles, topped
with seagulls pointing in the same direction, west
toward the setting sun:

a catalogue of clichés before she knew
cliché would overtake memory,
replace it with postcards.

———

But she had never come to Venice by sea.
Time to admit the unglamorous truth,
set the record straight.

After a month of seasickness
in a second-class cabin
from Djakarta to Genoa,

she took the shabby
train ride through monochrome farmland
pocked with desolate factories, terminating

in the fascist-modern Venezia stazione.
With the horde of camera-strung day-trippers
she rode the suffocating bus-boat

along the grand canal,
her mother sighing—ecstatic—
past the miles of moldy stucco.

When she stepped off the gang
plank at the Accademia vap stop
her batik shift blew up,

eliciting a whistle—at age twelve,
her first whistle—the words *che scandolo signorina!*
more compliment than reprimand.

The first night on the fold-out couch at her sister's
damp ground-floor apartment on Rio San Trovaso
she's almost

forgotten, but the cough born of mold,
dirt, and plaster refuses erasure. As does
the whistle.

RIALTO

Invisible in this cheap night scene of the familiar bridge
the lives—the lies—we lived
on both sides of the canal,

invisible the water's stench at low tide,
the rotting debris beneath
the picture-perfect surface,

invisible the adjacent market still smelling
of fish and ammonia, its slime of scales
adorning the ground,

invisible, too, in this souvenir print, the inevitable
rat crouched under the pilaster, his throat
quivering benignly in the moonlight,

the silvery glow
a local specialty: filth
disguised as ornament.

ROOFTOP: AERIAL VIEW

She is twelve, an expat brat
in a bikini, sunbathing
on a rooftop terrace. His terrace.

He is her first Jewish Intellectual,
a young scholar on a Fulbright
photographing Venetian churches.

Today, on the sly, he photographs *her*.
It is not important. Only the sun
is important, the bikini stencil it burns

around her budding breasts,
the terrace. There are fresh cherries too, and ice tea:
so American she feels, so reassuringly American

and adult, drinking ice tea, speaking English on the rooftop,
at ease in a bikini, spitting
pits into a green Murano dish.

She is comfortable with men.
Expecting the worst (three brothers had seen to that)
she is never let down.

He feeds her books and talk. She learns
smart is sexy. The eros of mind thrills her.
He throws out the line, reels her in.

Some days more than others she feels his appetite, his eyes
on her, the camera, a reach—inadvertent
brush of skin on skin.

From the bedroom window his wife watches them.
Her head aches.
The sun's too bright, says the wife, then

ducks inside, whipping her wet hair into a black rope,
twisting it at the nape against her stark-white skin.
She has a patrician voice and is forever saying things like

*That would look nice
on Jake, where
might I find one like that for Jake?*

From him never a word about Kitty.
That is her name, Kitty. With a
feline grace and diffidence to match.

What Kitty thinks the girl does not know.
What she knows is the terrace, the camera, the books,
the endless boredom of summer which abruptly

one day ends when on the stairwell
a team of medics passes her, running
Kitty on a stretcher to the nearest canal.

No Jake in sight to ride with her
in the ambulance boat. No Jake
to loosen the knot at her neck.

At home, no explanation. Nothing
about headaches, nothing about the rope or the pills,
nothing except *no more rooftop young lady*

(a punishment? a censure?)
and overheard,
the incomprehensible word: *breakdown.*

For the girl not only the season is broken, but
her summer flirtation,
the rooftop bond that is not a bond.

The Americans disperse, most
to different continents—leaving Venice, then later
returning (together, apart) year after

year returning and returning—
changed and unchanged
to the same city which never changes.

Later, when she is Kitty's age and back in their city,
she hears again that patrician voice
whining behind her on the riva:

The sun's too bright. The girl
—for she feels herself suddenly to be the girl
in the bikini on the terrace—turns

to answer the person who may or may not be Kitty
and sees everything—the indelible rooftop, the bikini,
the books consumed with ice tea and cherries, Jake's camera

probing, then retreating, her knowing innocence, Kitty's
tight black twist, the careless pits
spit into the green Murano dish.

PACT, 1968

You blew in like an autumn breeze
gentle and steady
from across the eastern seas—
not to save us
(that wasn't in your power)
but to set us straight, cool
us down from our wild summer.
In your absence Mother regressed,
became Sister,
like me a fatherless vagabond
out of school burning
with adolescent wanderlust.
From Venice to Ravenna to Rome to Capri
and back, all summer hitchhiking
up and down the coasts,
we relished our fleabag frugality
and Via Veneto splurges,
two girls gambling
with their looks to get rides
and winning. She swore
me to secrecy, brazen
but ashamed.

That October in Venice you arrived
too late
with your fatherly admonitions.
Modesty bored me.
I'd sworn my allegiance
to excess
and the sisterhood of lies.

MOON WALK
July 20, 1969

It is midnight on earth.

The Venice station, by now
half dreamscape / half memory
in the wake of my first breakup,

is empty. Night mist rising from the canals.

The usual bustle
of vendors and tourists
gone.

I am alone.

Just in on the train from Paris,
adrift, broke and fighting panic,
I am midway through my sixteenth summer

at home, but not, in the deserted city.

Walking the circular streets
across town to Castello
—my old orbit—

TV light spilling out windows my only guide,

I look for and find the old address.
trentanove dodici
trentanove dodici

Eccolo: trentanove dodici!

Little has changed. The old neighbors are still
the old neighbors; I ring
the bell next to their brass name plate.

I ascend the stairs

to the rooftop apartment where,
deferring to the television,
Jake and his new wife embrace me in silence.

I am no longer the enticing child he once knew

and girls in their teens do not draw him. The past and our reunion
after three years seem unimportant compared to the slow-
motion drama playing out on the screen.

Mesmerized

we wordlessly watch the hazy specter
of a man in a space suit
bouncing   floating   over the dunes

Hypnotic shots of a lunar landscape:

Walter Cronkite anchors the scene
as the module Eagle descends
to a surface littered with boulders

—*The Sea of Tranquility*—

then drifts
and lands softly
on something like sand.

magnificent   desolation   giant   step

The words crackle down to us
with the solitary image,
our weightless flag planted there, grainy and gray,

against all odds   against gravity.

The reel loops
and we are up in the air
drifting again

over and over in the module,

surveying again
the sci-fi future passing already
into our mythic past.

Jake breaks the spell, calls me *Purg!*

short for Purgatory, the name my brothers coined
to taunt their too-pious sister with the fact
that we are sinners and as sinners we must burn.

Unmoored, adrift—abandoned,

or just released?
I step out alone
onto the rooftop,

take in the real moon above and its cold glow below

in the watery street that is not a street, this otherworldly place
my refuge, my home. Was it Dante who reserved
the first sphere of heaven—the moon—for the vow breakers?

CANZONCINO: AIR FOR MY FATHER

We are gliding below the clouds,
to my right the lighted wing.
Beneath it, tiny lights on the lagoon,

black grit of the mainland,
then the fish map of Venice, its terra-cotta puzzle pieces
fitting into an improbable whole.

I am listening to Nathan Milstein, your
contemporary, play the Tchaikovsky violin concerto.
The second movement—sweet, unbearable—

followed by the steady rise towards a frenetic end
as our landing gear slides into place with a jolt.
The plane careens and dips.

Allegro vivacissimo.
The city beneath us suddenly sideways, then
under us

as we straighten out, regain balance, hit ground.
Hysteria in the harmonics; sanity,
dark and continuous, restored in the baseline.

Blue, white, and yellow fireflies
blink their SOS
outside my window.

Inside: the *Finale* with its bombastic resolution.

I am impervious to its triumph.

I do not accept your final silence.

URN

I dreamt of your ashes filling
an enormous Venetian urn, cloudy
cerulean-blue glass encasing yellow flecks, blown
according to an ancient Roman method. Instead of standing upright
on the floor, it reposed on a kind of altar in Mamita's hospital room surrounded
by rosaries and crucifixes, beneath a framed picture of Saint Francis's prayer,
the one in which he asks to become oh lord an instrument of peace even
as violence thrashes about him. I grabbed the rim and tipped it over,
spilling its contents to the ground: instead of ashes, salt—a sea
of solid tears scattering chaotically over the terrazzo.
Among the grains, as if from an explosion, shreds
of your blue hospital robe, pale blue
like your eyes, tattered remnants
of your last days littering
your body's remains,
refusing to settle.

III

AMBITION OF SAND

Submerged in the alluvial lagoon, adrift
but content in my sedimentary ways,
you found me:

a crush of inert coral, silica-lime and shell.
Under your feet I pumiced the callus, smoothed
the surface of arch and heel, ground

my way to the intimate space between toe and toe—
Oh, to reside there like nacre in the fold:
this was my modest desire.

But when you slipped me into your pail, the hard touch of tin
dry and cold against my wet grains
hardened something inside me, awakened

the old hunger for an igneous future I thought
to have tamed. Back
came the obsidian dreams troubling my infant sleep,

the volcanic longing
for something, someone
to change me—

from silt
to liquid
to lava—

Empty me into the furnace till I melt
then pick me from the flame and blow me
till I burst into globes transparent and airy alight on your pole.

Fill me. Don't cool me.
Burn me
and turn me

again and again.   Spin me.   Stay in me.

Spin—
spin me into glass.

AT THE GUGGENHEIM MUSEUM, VENICE

I am straddling Marini's horse,
using the horseman's cock as my handle,
galloping in place until it comes off in my hand.

It is a dry stone thing—nothing obscene—
just portable.
Across the canal my husband waves from our apartment terrace,

laughing at my handful. Inside,
Modigliani ladies look on with
dignified, elongated restraint while

Carrà's profile, square, and compass
suggest parameters for measureless passion:
Here, even enigma knows its limits.

Above striving, Mrs. Guggenheim's white palazzo squats
on its haunches, alert
but at rest, refusing

filigrees, minarets, or mosaic,
its only ornament the water, the light.
In the garden her departed poodles sleep

their permanent sleep beneath the blue
shade of a rare pine beside
a still rarer fountain.

I am in Venice
in a dog cemetery
holding a useless stone cock.

Am I wasting my life?

LIDO

The old woman in the chaise stares at the sky, imagines clouds,
definition where instead there is only emptiness—blue and unforgiving.
Her gold necklace leaves dents on her loose leather chest.

She listens to the raucous children playing ball,
screaming in German or French or Italian;
they are all trilingual in the adjacent *capanna*.

She imagines herself shoveling sand, packing
it flat, smoothing with the shovel
so not one crease remains.

The sand is the skin of the beach.
Dry and old
as God. She is alone, but not alone.

Her man is walking along the water's edge,
enjoying the topless beauties basking on the pier,
their hard nipples bobbing in conversation with the sun.

She remembers the eyes of men on her once plump breasts.
It was not entirely unpleasant.
But very tiring. Even then.

The attendant in his white shorts and yellow cummerbund
adjusts the awning overhead,
brings her a pail of water to rinse her feet. And waits.

She nods and begins her end-of-day ablutions—
cool water on her painted toes,
gritty towel on her back,

breeze picking up over the lagoon and the sand
sinking to the pail bottom
telling her it's time.

When her husband returns, aroused from his sightseeing,
will she indulge or refuse him?

TRAMONTO

     Go on. Weep. Look east
to the footage of the Fenice burning,
flames filling the monitor, and go on,
mourn the molten filigree disappearing
inside, tiers of gold leaf ringing the room,
rows of red velvet feeding the fire.
Mourn the hours—no, years—
of enchantment, the spell of arias
and scenery, enactments of love,
the opera of our daily lives, yesterday's
pleasures—consumed.

     Or look west to the place
where earth and sun for the moment align,
across the lagoon and between the mountains,
tra i monti, relish the setting Venetian sun
as it finishes tormenting the Armenian monks
on the island of San Lazzaro as it once crazed
the *manicomio* inmates of San Servolo.

     Quick now, before it's gone, look
through that needle-narrow aperture between
the islands, threading its way to the mainland:
fasten your sight to the last rays of the day,
to the refracted light on the horizon—catch
the green flash—

And before another day
of summer miasma overtakes us, tell yourself
the same reassuring lie:

> *Another day together, safe.*
> *The mirage—insist on this—is real.*

AT SEA

Drowning again, sucked
into the undertow of the quotidian.

I am whirling inside the wave, my feet
flipped up like a whale's tail.

I sound for you but there is no answer.
You are near, but invisible.

I have almost found you.
I know this the way I know

that you are not dead,
just lost. Or is it I who am drowning

in my own dull panic and you
who are trying to save me?

A silent cough floats above me, a shimmering
bubble that could only be yours,

and in that bubble your bewildered face.
I swim to you and am absorbed.

My hair spreads out like seaweed,
enfolds us both.

La Serenissima, indifferent to harmony as she is to discord,
glimmers blind from the distant shore.

CALLAS IN VENICE

"The penalty for all will be death
if the Prince's name is not discovered by morning."
—*Turandot*

Our neighbor at Borgo Loco works late at the casino. Nightly,
at three, his croupier feet rake across the tiled floor
above us, the heavy tread dragging from room
to room to room. Not a trace of the roulette
wheel's agile spin, the pearl's
light bounce from
red to black
to red.

As he readies for bed, drawers open and close, doors slam.
Gestures belonging to a sizeable man, thickset
and burly, not the slender, tuxedoed master
I picture dealing blackjack, stone cold
as he silently passes you your chips,
daring you to stand,
double your bet,
or surrender.

He storms from north to south, east to west, mapping every
inch of the place as if to reorient himself, shake off
the hours enabling loss at the gambling table.
Once he's stomped off his stress and flushed
away what remains of worry and waste,
he hurls onto the rusty springs
over our heads
and rests.

Under the casino where our croupier works nightly, the Wagner
Museum will open by day with a display of Maria Callas *objets*:
costumes, programs, and photos from the Venice years.
All over Venice Callas's diva half smile beckons us
to the exhibition. At Rialto she winks from a fish
market column. On a banner near la ferrovia
she dares tourists to skip the stale
attractions, visit her instead.

Outside the Accademia she's plastered on a trash can, coffee grounds
spilling onto her forehead. A line of ragu bisects her perfectly
arched left eyebrow but does nothing to mar her beauty—
the high cheek bones, the *sempre divina* gaze.
Across her chin, scrawled indelibly
in blue marker, this graffiti:
Look what you've done
to my song.

At the casino tonight, above the museum where Callas's photos
and costumes lie in state, the gamblers arrive charged to win,
destined to lose. We spot our croupier presiding now over
card craps. No wheel, no dice. Intent on outwitting
the house at a game we know, we sit at his table.
But here, as at home, he tramples over
our timid pass-line bets until
we buckle and fold.

Back at Borgo Loco we lie sleepless, defeated. To calm ourselves we sing
snatches of arias, call up images and scraps from the museum vitrines:
Aida's bejeweled belt coiled around a photo of Callas at the Lido,
her legs sprawled on the industrialist Meneghini's fat lap.
Was she wearing the bikini framed on the wall,
its delicate white breast cups
joined by an elegant
silver ring?

Still, sleep eludes us. In its place dread, the usual vigil
for the nightly stampede. But tonight when
our nameless croupier returns, he is quiet.
No pounding. Instead, he throws open
the doors to his balcony, steps
into the dark and sings
(to whom? to me?)
Nessun dorma!

His clear tenor rings out onto the desolate campo, ricochets
through the mist, from decayed wall to decayed wall.
I lie still, alert to his serenade, letting
the sweet timbre of his voice wash
over me. Do I wake or do
I sleep? Will he,
at last, reveal
his name?

Is he Calàf, my suitor?
Shall I marry—
or kill him?

LA TEMPESTA

after a painting by Giorgione

For years we told ourselves we might avoid it,
as if it hadn't been there all along, buried
beneath the ruins we thought quaint, picturesque.

Even the lightning crashing menace across the sky
we refused to take seriously.

Instead, we bought the souvenir tie in the museum shop
and laughed at how, out of context, the electric
streak adorning it was

just a smear of yellow across an expanse of lagoon-green silk,
the rest of the story brewing
offstage, out of view.

Like Giorgione, we trained our focus on the lush foreground
(woman nursing infant by stream; handsome voyeur eyeing her),
preferring to ignore the rest:

the deaths accumulating among the old and the unlucky young,
illnesses and overdoses claiming them relentlessly
with each passing season.

But the ruins in the distance—the dilapidated bridge to the approaching
    night—pull us with a steady, patient
insistence

toward the lightning, the inexorably tormented sky.

So we gather our cloaks—
not against the storm (which *will* arrive)
but against our dread of the storm.

AUBADE

Silence, then the boatman's cry.

Oar slash through water; at the wall
a thud, muffled hull against stone.
The usual depths, beckoning—

Then life-sounds cancelling the call:
rat-scuttle off the bridge,

the sound of bickering. Last night's lost
newlyweds still wandering,
each blaming the other.

Dawn eases in with no bird song:
only the sarcastic seagull's crow-caw,

pigeon flutter in the eaves, then
early light-dust pushing
through the shutter crack colonizing the furniture.

I had been dreaming of my soul.
Somehow I had managed to misplace it.

Now morning erupts with a fracas of bells
obliterating thought and—for the moment—
the concomitant dark.

WHAT I MEANT TO SAY: IN MEMORY OF
MICHAEL MAZUR, 1935–2009

I never think of you in August.

So now, though you love Venice and we're just in on the early train,
already fighting the day-tripping August mob,
I'm not thinking of you.

In Cambridge it's still night and probably cool, but here in Venice
we're so hot we forget how sick you've been, or how we missed
seeing you last time we were in town. We don't think

about you or anyone. It's too hot
for thought. Intent on reaching the hotel, we plow on ahead, up
Strada Nuova; we don't even look at the new Calatrava bridge spanning

the canal, or at the canal itself shimmering its greasy reflections.
We barely notice the churches with their bronze plaques
promising quattrocento treasures behind rough brown facades.

We pass them by—too hot, too bored, too jaded
from years of countless returns
to this city we both know by heart.

The churches, we say,
the churches of Venice have never seemed
as weirdly plain, as homely—downright ugly—as they do today

in the positively tropical heat, in the positively godforsaken
barren stretch of stone and backwater clothesline-infested
pigeon-shit-covered-campo-after-dead-end campo.

What's that about?
I always meant to ask you.
Maybe it's because the city—most of it,

I hear myself telling you—is so goddamn gorgeous it was
a form of prayer for the odd builder to renounce ornament
for the walls of god's house. So much for theory, I think,

as we drag up in front of Santa Maria dei Miracoli,
that tiny jewel of a perfect marble temple
in Cannaregio with not one painting of interest inside

to distract from its external white and pink resplendence—
you know the one I mean: the one with the gilded cupola atop
an off-kilter bell tower listing flirtatiously toward the canal.

We always come to it in its otherwise drab, cramped quarters
as upon a Lilliputian mirage, crossing
one of those ponti storti that fork out

in two directions onto a churchlet island, astonished.
In this heat it has no right
to delight. But it does, brazenly.

How is that? I never asked and you never said.

On days like this, walking clear across town to the Giardini,
sucking ices to survive, keeping to the interior,
did you avoid the Riva ablaze in the heat,

as we do, shunning
the open patch of white stone burning
before that run-down palazzo

where you lived for a year when you were a kid
with an Italian host family? Remembering the story
—about that time, about their daughter?—we turn

from the shady backstreet and head straight for the red brick façade
of what's now a hotel and stare, retrieving what we can
of the tale: some expectation, a disappointment maybe, not a scandal

but enough for you to tell it with some mix of rue and amusement, nothing
to diminish your sense of this city as a kind of home
to which you return again and again.

But this is more my compulsion, not yours—to be here for every Biennale
no matter the heat, no matter the awfulness of what we come back each time
to see: the Giardini pavilions basting in the sun, a park hardly a park, consecrated

to someone's idea of art, the selected dreck of nations.
At this point I *am* thinking of you, remembering
how the one time you were invited to exhibit at the Biennale

you refused, joining a group of Vietnam protesters who then
behind your back
exhibited anyway.

I'm thinking of you and actively wishing you were here
to help us process what we're seeing, to temper our disdain
at the miles of stale installations,

acres of exhausted Duchampian crap, recherché ironies
and ready-made profundities. Would some sense of guild honor
have allowed you to take it all in without scorn?

In my dreams I defend my dismissals with articulate rage and superior wit.
But in truth, before you, I am usually mute,
riding out your hilarious blue streak. No sacrifice to listen.

By now it's noon in Cambridge,
sunset where we are,
and I need to ask you—*today*—

what you think—what you'd have thought—
of the Spain pavilion
with the huge milky landscapes of Barceló

whose work, though he is Catalán and resides in Africa, reminds me
of yours. How to take in his radiographic lithos without thinking
of your own eerie x-ray prints? Or his large ceramic vessels without imagining

them as tributes to your own rocks-in-water paintings,
those stubborn totems of resilience,
stalwart against the painted current?

———

Hours later, nighttime in the Hotel Giorgione
I turn on my laptop and see the *Globe*'s online obit:
your stylized blossoms in purple and pink fairly leap

off my monitor and I think,
not for the last time, that there's something
I need to ask you about them—all those flowers,

everywhere in your drawings and paintings—cyclamen, calla lilies, irises—all those icons of relentless vitality now suddenly anomalous in this city of water and stone.

DREAM OF THE CHALICE

after Sereni

Evening seeps into the glass, filling
it steadily even as you bring it to your thirsty lips,
and sip, then hold the glass to mine. Back and forth,
we sip and share, draining the cup to the dregs. Still,
the night pours in and still our thirst—how is it
undiminished? No fear of endings or loss, only
the steady back-and-forth, ceaselessly requited.
The cup empties and the cup fills.
Someday they will say:
what a love that was!
Meanwhile,
the bells
of Santa
Maria
Formosa
sound the vespers, spread
their melancholy cheer across the piazza.
Together, we balance the chalice, hold it steady.
Yet with each toll a little splash escapes, slips off the rim.
We remember the rule, tighten our grip, but to no avail:
what is spilled will not refill.

FONDAMENTE NOVE

Ogni Santi—Feast of All Souls

All wrong, this late October heat, all wrong.
Summer sun persisting, refusing to finish.
Shops flung open for the business of burial,
selling funerary sculpture, condolence bouquets,
all of it overflowing with Titian reds, Tintoretto blues—
the pretty souvenirs of the dead.

Widows chat with florists and stonecutters;
their black-stocking grief donned daily
as they ride with friends to San Michele
to lay flowers at their husbands'
graves. *Tutto bene*
they reassure one another

on the boat home, admiring
each other's smart afternoon attire.
This routine living well off the dead,
this cheerful prosperity
along the desolate embankment—
why does its sanity not console me?

We need the cold
to resume with its white chill.
Sail in, north wind, blow
through and renew
our incurable bereavement.
We want nothing of summer or recovery.
Allow us our lunatic winter.

THE JEWISH CEMETERY, LIDO

Behind brick walls
and high wrought iron gates
the seeds of the world blow in,

gather and grow,
their offspring now custodians
of the twice-exiled ghetto dead.

Over the gravestones
English ivy wraps
the Chinese hibiscus, then hurls

itself over the Levi family headstone,
its jug and basin emblem a reminder
of their temple-washing rituals. Adjacent:

the priestly Cohan tomb
with its crest of hands blessing
in turn the ones who wash them.

Over them unfurl vines,
green and purple Wandering Jews, covering
the graven image,

the sin Venetian rabbis once allowed,
a quattrocento easement for Jews drunk
like goyim on art:

the D'Angeli family
punning predictably
with carved stone angels

while the Sullums choose as their attribute
a staircase—*sulám* in Hebrew, close enough. Nearby,
Samson slays the lion on the Cividal and Merari sarcophagi,

shofars and torahs plentiful as crosses at San Michele,
images still legible where words are not.
Over here the poet Sarra Copio Sullam is buried

with her five languages, her poems,
and all her famous arguments
with the great intellects of her time.

There lies Leone da Modena, guarded
by cypresses and twisted American wisteria,
his book on Jewish ritual long forgotten.

In 1329 a certain Samuel, about whom nothing is known
except that he was the son of Dr. Shomshon,
was buried here. Probably he was a lender,

a banker allowed to circulate by day, but by night confined
to the ghetto, a *usurer* tolerated in the lagoon city
only for his money, reviled by the Christians who needed it.

Behind the wall
Jews trading with Jews:
rag traders, dye workers, merchants in oil

or wine, and inn keepers for vagrants,
for refugees from the Inquisition,
for the People of the Book.

In the desolate square of the Ghetto Novo you can see them still
through the porticos to the bare circular clearing
with all its houses facing in. Forbidden the outer view,

they turn inward. And their banished dead, rowed out and away
across the lagoon, avoiding bridges so the rabble
won't pelt them with stones and curses,

end here now with the vacationing rich
on the Lido where the diaspora of seeds has landed, rooted
and grown careless as the irrelevant tea roses

which, once hunted down in Russia and harvested for sequins, now
mate freely and spread, purging and renewing from season to season,
tumbling heedlessly over the tombs.

BRODSKY AT SAN MICHELE, 1996

That endless night in December—with six weeks to live—
you discourse, Joseph, from our Eames chair,
grandiloquent with vodka.

Verse, verso.

With each spoken line break, a drag
from your cigarette, your left hand swings
back and forth, lips
to ashtray and back again.

To hell with forecasts of your failing heart.
Your right hand rakes the rug,
fingers score imaginary rows,
scrape at words,

coughing heedlessly as you plow on, harrow-hand
tilling the text—*We till
and we sow,
one line, then another.*

As if the literal body could drag on
forever, follow the metaphor, harvest the words.

———

By summer, back in Venice, we make
our pilgrimage to your grave, crossing

the lagoon to the walled island of the dead,
just one stop away from the islands of the living.
No breeze or rain for weeks.

We step onto the half-submerged embankment
where flood and drought cohabit, past
walls of graves stacked like drawers
to the hedged-in garden reserved
for the well-heeled dead.

The evergreens are brown and
the palm fronds, dropping, bow to the heat.

Christ everywhere: crucified, resurrected,
with saints and without.
Still no tombstone.

We rake your grave, wipe clean
your name and dates,

the rude letters carved onto two crossed sticks stabbed
precariously into the ground. A cross
for you, *traditore,*

to mark—or mock?—
your final translation:

exiled from Jews, but restored
to the Russians, Diaghilev and Stravinsky—
on the same island at least.

How shrewd then, the move:
interred at last near your Christian peers,

a place where a Jew has no place
—*furbone!*—
across from Black Shirt Ezra,

now sentenced
to endure you for eternity.

The sandy dirt is dry and hard, the poppies
in the vase black with mold. And the vines—
there are no vines.

The parched myrtle covering
other plots has not yet grown over yours.

I sweep away the debris, order
scattered love notes from fans, sticky
offerings of Russian candies, dead rose-stems.

I put stones on the mound and instead of Kaddish
recite the only lines of yours I know by heart:

I sit at my desk.
My life is grotesque.

TO FORGET VENICE

for Mimi (1918-2012)

Maybe it's the getting lost that brings me back,
the seeming to know every street, campo, canal,
hurtling down a familiar path only to end abruptly at water,
having to retrace my steps, turn, then turn again,
looking for the beginning but finding only that it's gone,
not there at all: vanished. That bridge

I traversed hours ago is not the bridge
I cross now suddenly in a panic to get back
to where I started. The old butcher shop is gone.
So, too, Marcon's latteria facing the canal—
another landmark—gone. I open the map again,
finger follow the maze to get my bearings. Water,

water everywhere—I stop at a bar to buy water
but refuse to ask directions, reach into the fridge
for a Pellegrino, pay the barman, and set out again,
this time following signs to the station, back
to my beginning. At the next bridge I spot a patch of Grand Canal
and, ah, to the left, Rio San Trovaso, the gondola workshop, *lo squero*—not gone!—

its yard littered with boat carcasses to be repaired or junked for spare parts. Gone
now for *ferragosto*, the workers will soon reopen its boat-wide doors to the water,
thrusting restored gondole out onto the choppy sun-drenched canal
facing Giudecca. I imagine their path as they ride the waves' ridge
into the horizon. Calming to see them recede. No turning back—
each wave rolling away, seen again and then hypnotically again

lost to the sea. The getting lost, giving into it, finding my way again—
seduction and submission. Antique pleasure. By now the panic's gone.
Inside the cycle of Eternal Return there's peace. Inside the always going-back-
repetition-compulsion-to-return is refuge, a kind of being-lost amniotic water,
its fluid unknowing lifting me up, two wooden steps at a time, over the Accademia bridge,
focused always on the return, charging forward yet back, ignoring the Grand Canal,

its Main Street bustle below me, threading to the interior, past canal
after canal as my own interior relentlessly unreels the familiar scenes again:
my mother pushing a baby carriage, two granddaughters in hand, bridge over bridge.
Story over story, our memories mingling, misremembered. Now ancient, mostly gone
in the head, she fills in her thin present with vanished incident: the spilled water
episode a favorite, my sister's accident, lied about for years. Now we're back

to that rare snow day in Venice, begun with enchantment, my sister back
from her walk, lit with benediction—every snow-covered canal
a gift of grace—comes home to her husband's command to immediately boil water
for the diapers. In her haste to obey she spills the pot onto her legs. Later and again
we said it was for pasta, masking her servility. Our shame like her burn still not gone.
Proust, who knew about lies, remembered—or imagined—the bridge

I now see from my window and everything before and after it: his relentless bridge
to Albertine, to regrets over the unpurchased Fortuny dress, to Combray and back
to Venice, the perfect match for his serpentine mind, there then gone
down another path, winding around and around, pausing to contemplate a canal,
then back to the Guermantes, losing the point, then finding it again,
the pleasure endlessly, lovingly deferred, not diluted by this water

but intensified, reflected and multiplied, his life his prose, this water
the very prose he swam and drowned in, each intricate thought a bridge
to another, each desire engendering a new hunger to look back
to an old obsession, only to pursue the course again
through the inexorable maze of his imagination, each tangled canal
opening onto a new memory to explore, record, consume before it's gone.

Time the prey. Each search a hunt. Somewhere he recalls riding in a gon-
dola, gliding along the Grand Canal, flanked by buildings doubled in water,
the "chain of marble cliffs" he remembers from Ruskin, picturesque as a Canal-
etto and above, the elegant women waving from the bridge,
dressed to the nines for the daily *passeggiata* display. Again
he calls up *petite maman* and the drifting—just so—with her, back

when she was young and he younger, her slender back
upright seated on the velvet chair in front of him—her image never gone—
gliding in a gondola down the Grand Canal. As with me and my own mamita—again,
she appears, inserting herself everywhere, lost and then found, like water
coursing through this city she circulates endlessly, our common past the bridge
we cross together when I call: *Remember when Laura almost ran into the canal?*

Once she was water and bridge to me, the connecting force and the canal
flowing steadily beneath. When she is lost it will be time to begin again, back
at the beginning: *For a long time I used to go to bed early*—Marcel's sleepy bridge
to the past now her present. Bedridden in Miami at 93, her mind nearly gone,
she nobly fakes remembering, distracts me shrewdly by asking for water,
please, covering dementia with thirst. Months later, from Venice, I call again

on my birthday, as always. Again I rehearse old times, our view of the canal, then
and now, the lagoon-green water, the daily walk to Rialto bridge, her memories mixed
with mine. We talk it back. The past: lost, retrieved, ever receding, then again gone.

NOTES

p. 17, "To Lenin from Venice": Nadezhda Krupskaya married Lenin in 1898, but the couple was often separated because of their respective arrests, imprisonment, and exile. Lenin was in Italy in 1908 for a period. This poem imagines that they were together and that she was left behind when he returned to Russia.

p. 36, "Moon Walk": Actual memory combined with recent viewings of archival footage available online moved me to name Walter Cronkite as the anchorman of the Apollo moon landing I would have seen in Venice in 1969. But of course that was impossible; the anchorman I would have seen that summer on Italian television was Tito Stagno. The words "magnificent desolation ... giant step ... " would have been heard in Italian: "desolazione magnifica ... passo gigantesco."

p. 51, "Tramonto": On January 29, 1996, the most important opera house in Venice, La Fenice, burned to the ground, probably as the result of arson. It had been built originally on the site of the San Benedetto Theater when that older building burned down in 1774. The new theatre was therefore named *Fenice*, for the phoenix, whose fate it is to rise from the ashes of its predecessor. Over the course of its history the Fenice has burned down several times and then returned, restored; its most recent reconstruction was concluded in December 2003.

p. 54, "Callas in Venice": This poem is dedicated to Rosella Mamoli Zorzi and Marino Zorzi.